Demy~~~~ ~~~~ ~~~~ French Grammar

Clarifying the Accents, Adjectives, Determiners, Questions/Negation, Pronouns, Tricky Prepositions, Imparfait/Passé Composé, & the French Subjunctive

Brandon Simpson
Small Town Press
Dry Ridge, KY

ISBN-13: 978-0-9816466-3-3
ISBN-10: 0-9816466-3-8

About the Author

Brandon Simpson has a B.A. in Spanish. In addition to Spanish, he minored in French and has also studied other languages as a hobby. He is the author of *Demystifying Spanish Grammar*, *Learning Foreign Languages*, and *Spanish Verb Tenses*. He currently keeps a blog at

http://foreign-language-enthusiasts.blogspot.com

He is also the founder of the Foreign Language Enthusiasts Yahoo group:

http://groups.yahoo.com/group/foreign_language_enthusiasts

He frequently visits the forum at

http://french.about.com

Disclaimer

Neither the author nor the publisher can be held liable for the misuse of this book. The explanations herein are merely here to help your comprehension of French grammar. Every possible effort was taken to ensure the accuracy of the information in this book. There may be, however, mistakes that neither the author nor the editors noticed. Some of the information in this book was provided by native speakers who are not necessarily experts of grammar. Reading this book will not guarantee mastery of the material nor will it guarantee a higher grade. This book is not endorsed by any company mentioned. The reader should also be aware that this book is not comprehensive. Readers should, and are also encouraged, to seek the advice of competent individuals.

Table of Contents

Introduction

As a French tutor, I am constantly asked the same questions by several students:

Why does this word have an accent?

Why *dans* and not *en*?

What is the difference between the *imparfait* and the *passé compose*?

The subjunctive? I give up!

I have tried to answer the majority of the questions I have heard in this book. As you read my explanations of French grammatical concepts, you will see that most grammatical concepts are not all that difficult when studied in isolation. However, when one or more grammatical concepts are mixed together, it can cause grammatical chaos. For that reason, I have included a chapter that will show you how to mix each concept in a systematic and logical manner.

This book is not intended for those with absolutely no background in French. It is better suited to students in intermediate or advanced French.

Accents

Many French students know where the written accents go, but they don't know why they go there. Others don't even write the accents because they don't think it makes a big difference; it does. You must write the accents because that's how the word is spelled. Omitting an accent is no different from omitting an entire letter.

In this chapter I have attempted to explain the rules to the accents with five basic rules. These rules probably don't encompass every possible reason, but they cover the majority.

L'accent aigu (é)

This accent mark only occurs over the vowel *e*. The French vowel *e* has three distinct pronunciations. When it is written with *l'accent aigu*, it is pronounced like the *ay* in *may*.

Example:

l'été	summer

L'accent grave (à,è,ù)

This accent mark occurs over the vowels *a* and *e*. When it is written over the *e*, it tells you that the *e* is pronounced like the *e* in *bed*. Its function is different when written over the vowels *a* and *u*. In this case, *l'accent grave* is used to differentiate two words that are spelled the same but with different meanings.

Examples:

a	has (3rd person singular conjugation of *avoir*)
à	at, to
ou	or
où	where
frère	brother
mère	mother

Le tréma

When there are two French vowels together, they usually create only one vowel sound, i.e. *mais (but)*. The *ai* in this word is pronounced like the *e* in *bed*. If we put a *tréma* over the *i*, the word is spelled *maïs (corn)* and pronounced *mah-ees*. Another example is *le Noël*, which is pronounced *noh-el*.

L'accent circonflexe

Nowadays, this accent mark really serves no purpose. It used to indicate that there was an *s*-sound afterward.

Examples:

l'âne	donkey
forêt	forest
l'île	island
l'hôpital	hospital
dû	*past part.* of devoir

Le cédille (ç)

The French letter *c* is pronounced [k] before the vowels *a, o,* and *u.* It is pronounced [s] before the vowels *e* and *i.* The *cédille* is only written before the vowels *a, o,* and *u.* Its functon is to tell you that the *c* is pronounced [s].

Examples:

ça	that/this
commençons	(we) begin
reçu	received (past participle)

Adjectives

An adjective is a word that modifies a noun. This chapter deals with descriptive adjectives (such as *green, big, old, etc.*). Demonstrative adjectives and possessive adjectives are explained in the chapter that deals with determiners. This chapter also discusses how French uses different constructions to modify a noun.

Descriptive Adjectives

There are two major differences between English and French adjectives. French adjectives *follow* the noun rather than precede it. (There are some adjectives that precede the noun. They'll be discussed later.) The other difference is that French adjectives must agree in gender and number with the noun they modify. Look at the following sentence:

J'ai une bleu voiture. – I have a blue car.
(incorrect)

In the first sentence, the adjective *bleu* is placed before the noun, and it does not agree with the gender of *voiture*. To make this sentence correct, we have to place the adjective *bleu* after *voiture*, and we have to add an *e* to make it feminine. The following sentence contains the corrections to the above sentence.

J'ai une voiture bleue. – I have a blue car.
(correct)

If the speaker has two cars, the sentence would be:

J'ai deux voitures bleues. – I have two blue cars.

In the previous sentence, we added both an *e* and an *s* to the adjective *bleu* because the noun *voitures* is feminine and plural. The following table contains the adjective *bleu* in all its forms.

	Singular	**Plural**
Masculine	bleu	bleus
Feminine	bleue	bleues

To make an adjective agree with its noun, do the following steps.

1. Identify the gender of the noun being modified.
   a. Add an −e if it's feminine.
2. Identify the number of the noun being modified.
   a. Add an −s if it's plural.

Of course, there are adjectives that do not follow this pattern. They follow other patterns:

1. If the adjective ends in *eau*, add *x* to the plural form. (The feminine form never ends in *eau*.)

	Singular	**Plural**
Masculine	beau	beaux
Feminine	belle	belles

2. If the adjective ends in *c*, add *he* to the feminine form.

	Singular	**Plural**
Masculine	blanc	blancs
Feminine	blanche	blanches

3. If the adjective already ends in *e*, adding another *e* is not necessary.

	Singular	Plural
Masculine	libre	libres
Feminine	libre	libres

4. If the adjective ends in *n*, add *ne* to the feminine form.

	Singular	Plural
Masculine	bon	bons
Feminine	bonne	bonnes

5. If the adjective ends in *eux*, change the *x* to *s* and add *e* to the feminine form. The masculine singular and plural forms are the same.

	Singular	Plural
Masculine	sérieux	sérieux
Feminine	sérieuse	sérieuses

6. If the adjective ends in *if*, the *f* changes to a *v* in the feminine form.

	Singular	Plural
Masculine	attentif	attentifs
Feminine	attentive	attentives

7. If the adjective ends in an *s*, it is not necessary to add another *s* to the masculine plural form.

	Singular	Plural
Masculine	français	français
Feminine	française	françaises

8. If an adjective ends in *al*, its masculine plural form ends in *aux*.

	Singular	Plural
Masculine	légal	légaux
Feminine	légale	légales

Adjectives that Precede the Noun

There is a small list of adjectives that precede the noun being modified. They're often called **BAGS** adjectives.

Beauty
Age
Goodness
Size

BAGS adjectives include, but are not limited to, the following:

French	English
beau	pretty, handsome
joli	pretty
mou	soft
vieux	old
jeune	young
nouveau	new
bon	good
mauvais	bad
grand	big
petit	small

As you can see, all these adjectives fit in the BAGS category. There are more BAGS adjectives than this, but this list covers the majority.

Since BAGS adjectives precede the noun, they may have more forms. There are five BAGS adjectives that have a special masculine-vowel form. This form is used when a masculine noun begins with a vowel or a non-aspirate *h*. Look at the following sentence.

C'est un vieux homme. – It's an old man.
(incorrect)

The adjective *vieux* must be changed to *vieil* because *homme* begins with a vowel sound. Here's the sentence with the correction:

C'est un vieil homme. – It's an old man.
(correct)

Here are charts of the five adjectives that have special masculine-vowel forms:

	Singular	Plural
Masculine	beau	beaux
Feminine	belle	belles
Masc.-vowel	bel	beaux

	Singular	Plural
Masculine	nouveau	nouveaux
Feminine	nouvelle	nouvelles
Masc.-vowel	nouvel	nouveaux

	Singular	Plural
Masculine	vieux	vieux
Feminine	vieille	vieilles
Masc.-vowel	vieil	vieux

	Singular	Plural
Masculine	fou	fous
Feminine	folle	folles
Masc.-vowel	fol	fous

	Singular	Plural
Masculine	mou	mous
Feminine	molle	molles
Masc.-vowel	mol	mous

Another case where an adjective may precede the noun is when the adjective is modifying a proper noun.

L'étonnant Spider-Man – the Amazing Spider-Man

Comparatives/Superlatives

Now that we have seen adjectives in their positive forms, we will learn how to express comparatives and extremes. In English, comparatives are formed by adding *er* to the end of most adjectives or by adding the adverb *more* before the adjective in question. Looking at the following:

Positive Form	Comparative Form
fast	faster
interesting	more interesting

There are also irregular comparative forms:

Positive Form	Comparative Form
good	better (*gooder* is not possible)
bad	worse (*badder* is not possible)

In French, to form the comparative form, the adverb *plus* is added before the adjective in question.

Positive Form	Comparative Form
vite (fast)	plus vite (more fast=faster)
intéressant (interesting)	plus intéressant (more interesting

In French, as in English, there are also irregular forms. Coincidentally, they are the same adjectives that are used in English.

Positive From	Comparative Form
bon	meilleur
mauvais	pire

The adjective must still follow the rules of gender and number. French also makes use of the structure *moins + adjectif*, which literally translates to *less + adjective*.

French	English
moins vite	less slow (faster)

To make a comparison of equality, English uses the structure *as + adjective + as*. French uses *aussi + adjectif + que*.

English	French
as + ADJECTIVE + as	aussi + ADJECTIF + que

Je suis aussi intelligent que vous.
I'm as smart as you.

Write the correct form of the comparative in the blank.

1. Mon chien est _____ que ton chien. (bon/plus)

2. Ce livre-ci est _____ que ce livre-là. (grand/plus)

3. La maison est _____ que les autres maisons. (petit/aussi)

4. Les ordinateurs des années soixante-dix sont _____ que ceux d'aujourd'hui. (lent/plus)

5. Les chats sont _____ que les chiens. (stupide/moins)

6. Le français est _____ que le russe. (joli/plus)

7. Les langues romances sont _____ que les langues slaviques. (joli/plus)

Translate the following sentences.

1. We have a bigger house than you (informal).

2. They have a more interesting book than us.

3. I have a smarter son than you (formal).

Invariable Adjectives

Invariable adjectives are adjective that do not change according to gender or number. They remain the same in all cases. The majority of invariable adjectives are actually nouns that eventually became used as adjectives. The first two invariable adjectives that beginning French students learn are the following: *orange* (orange) and *marron* (chestnut).

Examples:

J'ai des chevaux marron. – I have brown horses.
Mes cahiers sont orange. – My notebooks are orange.

(Note how *marron* and *orange* don't change.)
An adjective is also invariable if it follows one of the following words:

French	English
quelque chose	something
rien	nothing
quelqu'un	somebody
personne	nobody

When an adjective follows one these words, it is preceded by *de*.

French	English
quelque chose de bleu	something blue
rien de plus	nothing else/nothing more
quelqu'un d'autre	somebody else
personne d'important	nobody important

When the word *chose* stands alone, the adjective follows the regular rule:

French	English
une chose bleue	a blue thing

When the word *personne* means *person*, the adjective follows the regular rule:

French	English
une personne importante	an important person

Determiners

There are five types of determiners in French: definite, indefinite, partitive, demonstrative, and possessive. The definite determiner corresponds to *the* in English. The indefinite determiner corresponds to *a/an*. The partitive determiner has no direct translation in English. It usually translates as *some* or *any*.

The possessives and demonstratives are usually referred to as adjectives, but it is more logical to call them determiners. Why? In French it is possible to have the following structure:

Definite Determiner	Adjective	Noun
le	bon	livre

However, it is not possible to say the following two phrases:

French	English
le ce livre	the this book
le mon livre	the my book

Since the above two sentences are not possible, it makes more sense to separate the possessives and demonstratives from adjectives and classify them as determiners. If we use this classification, we can say that two determiners cannot accompany the same noun. Even though English follows the same rule, many beginning French students still say things like *ma la voiture*, even though they know that saying *my the car* is completely unacceptable in English.

Definite Determiners

	Singular	Plural
Masculine	le	les
Feminine	la	les
Vowel	l'	les

The definite determiner is used when the noun is used in the general sense and often with verbs of like or dislike.

Example:
J'aime le soda. – I like soda. (like)

Indefinite Determiners

	Singular	Plural
Masculine	un	des
Feminine	une	des
Vowel	-------------	des
Negative	de (d')	de (d')

The indefinite determiner is used when English uses *a/an*. It is usually used after *C'est*. It is not used with the verb *être* unless the adjective is being modified. When used in a negative sentence, the indefinite determiner becomes *de (d')*. This rule does not apply to the verb *être*. When *un* means *one*, *un* does not change to *de* in a negative sentence.

Examples:

French	English
C'est une voiture.	It's a car.
Ce n'est pas une voiture.	It's not a car.
Je suis professeur.	I'm a professor.
Je suis un bon professeur.	I'm a good professor.
Mon frère a un livre.	My brother has a book.
Mon frère n'a pas de livre.	My brother doesn't have a book.
Mon frère n'a pas un livre, plutôt deux.	My brother doesn't have one book, but rather two.

Partitive Determiners

	Singular	Plural
Masculine	du	des
Feminine	de la	des
Vowel	de l'	des
Negative	de (d')	de (d')

The partitive determiner refers to an unknown quantity of something. It usually translates to *some* or *any* in English.

When used in negative sentences, the indefinite and partitive determiners become *de (d')*. This rule does not apply to the verb *être*.

Examples:

French	English
Je voudrais du café.	I'd like some coffee.
Avez-vous de livres?	Do you have any books?
L'étudiant a des cahiers.	The student has some notebooks.
L'étudiant n'a pas de cahiers.	The student doesn't have any notebooks.

Translate the following sentences.

1. I see the car.
2. I don't see the car.
3. She wants a horse.
4. She doesn't want a horse.
5. They would like some coffee.
6. They don't want any coffee.
7. I don't have any money.
8. I don't have any money in my wallet.
9. That's a cat.
10. That's not a cat.
11. Are there any questions?
12. There aren't any questions.
13. The students want a party.
14. The students don't want a test.

Demonstrative Determiners

Demonstrative determiners correspond to the words *this/these* and *that/those* in English.

	Singular	Plural
Masculine	ce	ces
Feminine	cette	ces
Masc.-vowel	cet	ces

As you can see in the above table, all the plural forms are the same: *ces*. The feminine singular form is *cette*, and the masculine singular form is *ce*. However, if the following noun is masculine and begins with a vowel, *ce* becomes *cet*.

Since French does not make a clear distinction between *this* and *that*, it makes use of the following suffixes: *-ci* and *–là*.

Examples:

French	English
ce livre-ci	this book
ce livre-là	that book

Fill in the blanks with the correct demonstrative adjective.

1. Je veux lire _____ livre.

2. Elle veut _____ robe rouge.

3. Il parle à _____ homme.

4. Je vais lire _____ livres.

5. Elle a lu _____ livre.

6. Nous n'aimons pas _____ règles.

7. _____ chien est vieux.

8. _____ lumière est brillante.

9. _____ voitures sont en panne.

10. Je hais _____ cours (*sing).*

11. _____ ordinateur est très lent.

12. _____ ordinateurs sont très lents.

13. Je hais _____ cours (*plural).*

14. Qu'est-ce que tu fais dans _____ bâtiment-ci ?

15. _____ fois est la dernière fois.

16. _____ main est une terrible main de poker.

17. Voulez-vous _____ crayons-ci ou _____ crayons-là ?

Possessive Determiners

Possessive adjectives correspond to words such as *my, your, our,* etc.

	my	**your (tu)**	**his/her**
Masculine	mon	ton	son
Masc.-vowel	mon	ton	son
Feminin	ma	ta	sa
Plural	mes	tes	ses

	our	**your (vous)**	**their**
Singular	notre	votre	leur
Plural	nos	vos	leurs

There is nothing particularly mysterious about possessive determiners, but most students tend to use the singular possessive adjectives incorrectly. When they translate *his/her*, they use *son* for *his* and *sa* for *her*. This is, however, incorrect. The gender of the noun that the adjective is *modifying* is what determines which adjective to use.

Examples:
his car – sa voiture
her book – son livre

Translate the following.

1. my car
2. your book (informal)
3. her notebook
4. his shirt
5. our child
6. our children
7. your dictionary (formal)
8. your dictionaries (formal)
9. your books (informal)
10. their house
11. their houses
12. my cars

Questions/Negation

Making Questions

Making questions in French is not difficult, but doing so is difficult for most French students. In French, as in English and most languages, there are two types of questions: *yes/no* questions and information questions. A *yes/no* question is a question whose answer must be *yes* or *no*. An information question is a question whose answer can be any piece of information.

To learn how to form a yes/no question, use the acronym RIEN.

Rising Intonation
Inversion
Est-ce que
N'est-ce pas

Let's take the sentence *Vous parlez français* and turn it into a question with the four methods of making yes/no questions.

R	Vous parlez français?
I	Parlez-vous français?
E	Est-ce que vous parlez français?
N	Vous parlez français, n'est-ce pas?

Turn the following statements into questions by using all four methods.

1. Il est français.
2. Ils viennent.
3. Vous êtes des Etats-Unis.
4. Nous allons en France.
5. Elles ont la clé.

To make an information question, where the question must contain a question word, use the acronym PIE.

Place the question word at the end
Inversion
Est-ce que

For this example, we'll use the question *Where are you going?*

P	Vous allez où?
I	Où allez-vous?
E	Où est-ce que vous parlez?

Translate the following questions into French using all three methods.

1. Where are you from?
2. How many kids does he have?
3. Where does Marie work?

Questions with 3rd Person Subject

When a question has a 3rd person subject, there are two possibilities: a short form and a long form. When making a *yes/no* question, the long form is the only acceptable way. With an information question, either form is acceptable. However, it is better to use the long form.

Yes/No Question

French	English
Marie a-t-elle venue?	Did Marie come?

Information Question

French	English
Où ton frère habite-il?	Where does your brother live?

Negation

This section will deal with six negative adverbs in French.

French	English
ne...pas	(do) not
ne...jamais	never
ne...rien	nothing
ne...personne	nobody
ne...plus	no longer
ne...que	only
ne...guère	scarcely
ne...ni...ni	neither...nor
ne...nulle part	nowhere
ne...aucun(e)+NOUN	not any

As you can see from the chart, there are two components in French negative adverbs. The *ne* precedes the verb, and the second component follows the verb.

French	English
Je ne parle pas français.	I don't speak French.
Il ne regarde jamais la télé.	He never watches television.
Nous n'avons rien à cacher.	We have nothing to hide.
Tu ne peux plus regarder la télé.	You can no longer watch television.
Je ne vois personne.	I see nobody./I don't see anybody.
Elle n'a que cinquante dollars.	She only has fifty dollars.
Marie ne boit guère d'eau.	Marie scarcely drinks water.
Jacques n'aime ni le café ni la bière.	Jacques like neither coffee nor beer.
Je ne peux jamais trouver mes clés nulle part.	I can never find my keys anywhere.
L'étudiant n'apporte aucun livre avec lui en classe.	The student doesn't bring any book to class.

When *personne* and *rien* are the subject of a sentence, they are followed by *le ne explatif*. It's very common to omit *le ne explatif* in colloquial speech.

Personne ne me dit rien.
Nobody tells me anything.

Rien ne s'est passé.
Nothing happened.

Many French students may be tempted to conjugate the verb *faire* when making a negative sentence. This creates a direct translation:

Correct Way	Incorrect Way
Je ne sais pas.	*Je ne fais pas savoir.*

The correct French translation literally says *I know not.*

Pronouns

Pronouns in French behave as pronouns in English, but certain French pronouns do not follow the same rules or order as their English counterparts. There are also pronouns in French that do not exist in English.

In French, as in English, there are subject pronouns, direct object pronouns, indirect object pronouns, possessive pronouns, demonstrative pronouns, stressed pronouns and relative pronouns. French also makes use of adverbial pronouns, which do not exist in English.

Subject Pronouns

	Singular	Plural
1	je (j')	nous
2	tu	vous
3	il/elle/on	ils/elles

Since subject pronouns are essential to learning verb forms, French students learn how to use them in their first French course. So I will not go into great detail with them here, but I will clarify a few key points.

First, French has two second person pronouns: *tu* and *vous*. One is singular, and the other is plural. However, *vous* is used as the formal second person singular form.

The pronoun *on* has no direct translation in English. It could be translated as *one*, but English speakers use other pronouns instead.

French	English
Ici on parle français.	Here one speaks French.

Normally, an English speaker would say *Here we speak French*. But French uses *on*, also called the indefinite pronoun.

French	English
Comment dit-on ça en français?	How does one say this in French.

In this case, an English speaker would say *How do you say this in French?* However, the speaker is not asking *you* specifically how to say something in French. The speaker is asking how people in general say it in French.

Direct Object Pronouns

	Singular	**Plural**
1	me (m')	nous
2	te (t')	vous
3	le/la (l')	les

The direct object of a sentence receives the action of the verb.

Je regarde la télévision.

The subject is *je* (the doer of the action), and *la television* is the direct object (the recipient of the action).

Subject	**Verb**	**Direct Object**
Je	regarde	la télévision.

If we replace the direct object with a direct object pronoun, the sentence would be:

Je la regarde.

Subject	DO Pronoun	Verb
Je	la	regarde.

Rewrite the following sentences, replacing the direct objects with a direct object pronoun.

1. Nous savons la réponse.

2. J'aime l'ordinateur.

3. J'aime les ordinateurs.

4. Ils voient le chemin.

5. Détestez-vous cette voiture?

Indirect Object Pronouns

	Singular	Plural
1	me (m')	nous
2	te (t')	vous
3	lui	leur

The indirect object of a sentence is said to be the second recipient of the verb, but I find it easier to think of the direct object as the recipient of the direct object.

Je donne le livre à mon frère.

The subject is *je*, the direct object is *le livre*, and the indirect object is *mon frère*.

Subject	Verb	Direct Object	Indirect Object
Je	donne	le livre	à mon frère.

This sentence can be rewritten in three different ways:

Je le donne à mon frère.
(The direct object is replaced)

Subject	DO Pronoun	Verb	Indirect Object
Je	le	donne	à mon frère.

Je lui donne le livre.
(The indirect object is replaced.)

Subject	IO Pronoun	Verb	Direct Object
Je	lui	donne	le livre.

Je le lui donne.
(Both the direct object and the indirect object are replaced.)

Subject	DO Pronoun	IO Pronoun	Verb
Je	le	lui	donne.

Rewrite the following sentences, replacing the indirect object with an indirect object pronoun. Do not replace anything else.

1. Il parle à l'homme.

2. Nous donnons des cadeaux à nos enfants.

3. Vous parlez à Robert.

4. Ils parlent à Marie.

5. Je parle à mon professeur.

6. Il montre son tailleur à Chloé.

Possessive Pronouns

	MS	**FS**	**MP**	**FP**
mine	le mien	la mienne	les miens	les miennes
yours	le tien	la tienne	les tiens	les tiennes
his/hers/its	le sien	la sienne	les siens	les seines
ours	le nôtre	la nôtre	les nôtres	les nôtres
yours	le vôtre	la vôtre	les vôtres	les vôtres
theirs	le leur	la leur	les leurs	les leurs

Possessive pronouns in French behave much like their English counterparts. The difference is that the French possessive pronouns must agree in gender and number.

Ma voiture est rouge, mais la tienne est bleue.
My car is red, but yours is blue.

Instead of saying *ta voiture/your car* again, we simply use the possessive pronoun. Since *la voiture* feminine singular, we must use the feminine singular form.

Fill in the blank with the correct possessive pronoun.

1. Mes chaussures sont blanches, mais _____ (yours) sont noires.

2. Nos enfants sont grands, mais _____ (yours) sont petits.

3. Ses yeux sont verts, mais _____ (hers) sont bleus.

4. Vos étudiants sont intelligents, mais _____ (mine) sont un peu stupides.

Demonstrative Pronouns

	Singular	Plural
Masculine	celui	ceux
Feminine	celle	celles

Demonstrative pronouns replace demonstrative determiners. They correspond to *this one, that one, these ones,* and *those ones* in English.

Ce livre est très enneyeux, mais celui-là est intéressant.
This book is very boring, but that one is interesting.

It is required to add the suffixes −ci and −là to the end of the demonstrative pronoun. Remember that these suffixes are used to refer to *this* and *that*.

Fill in the blanks with the correct demonstrative pronoun.

1. Cette voiture est puissant, mais _____ est fragile.

2. Ce livre est grand, mais _____ est petit.

3. Ces cartes sont vielles, mais _____ sont nouvelles.

4. Ces chevaux sont bruns, mais _____ sont blancs.

Stressed Pronouns

	Singular	Plural
1	moi	nous
2	toi	vous
3	lui	eux
	elle	elles

These pronouns are used after the following:
>   -prepositions
>   -the words *et* and *que*
>   -the phrase *C'est*
>   -*être à* (to belong to)
>   -*faire attention à* (to pay attention to)
>   -*penser à* (to think about)
>   -*s'intéresser à* (to be interested in)

Examples:

J'ai quelque chose pour toi.
I have something for you.

Vous et moi sommes français.
You and I are French.

Elle a plus d'argent que vous.
She has more money than you.

C'est moi.
It's me.

Ce livre est à moi.
This book belongs to me.

Stressed pronouns are also used to place more emphasis on another pronoun or noun.

Moi, je suis ton père.
I *am your father.*

Translate the following sentences.

1. He and I have a lot of money.

2. We have something for you. (informal)

3. We have something for you. (formal)

4. The book belongs to me.

5. *She* is your cousin.

6. It's him.

7. She is prettier than her.

8. We have more money than you-all.

9. I want to go out with him.

10. He wants to go out with her.

Adverbial Pronouns (y & en)

The adverbial pronouns *y* and *en* have no English equivalent. *Y* is used to replace *à + thing* or *à/en + place*. *En* is used to replace expressions of quantity and *de + thing*. Since these are pronouns, they precede the verb.

Examples:

Subject	Verb	à/en + place
Je	vais	en France.
Subject	**Pronoun**	**Verb**
J'	y	vais.

Subject	Verb	à/en + place
Je	vais	au Japon.
Subject	**Pronoun**	**Verb**
J'	y	vais.

Subject	Verb	de+thing/quantity
Je	veux	du café.
Subject	**Pronoun**	**Verb**
J'	en	veux.

Subject	Verb	de+thing/quantity
Elle	a	deux frères.
Subject	**Pronoun**	**Verb**
Elle	en	a deux.

Subject	Verb	de+thing/quantity
Ils	ont	beaucoup de devoirs.
Subject	**Pronoun**	**Verb**
Ils	en	ont beaucoup.

Rewrite the following sentences with the correct adverbial pronoun.

1. Il y a deux livres.

2. Elle va au cinema.

3. Nous jouons au football.

4. L'université a beaucoup d'étudiants.

5. Il a trois frères.

6. Je voudrais du soda.

The pronoun *en* cannot replace *de + personne*. Instead, the person would be replaced by a stressed pronoun.

Il est jaleux de son frère.
Il est jaleux de lui.

Tricky Prepositions

Verb + Preposition + Infinitive

Many verbs are followed by a preposition when followed by an infinitive, usually *de* or *à*. There doesn't seem to be any rhyme or reason to why French uses one or the other. One general rule you can use is that *de* "looks back" and *à* "looks forward." Please keep in mind that this rule is very general.

French	English
Elle a commencé à manger à 5h.	*She started eating at 5 o'clock*
Elle a terminé de manger à 6h.	*She finished eating at 6 o'clock.*

Verb + Preposition + Noun

This section deals mainly with the structure *verb + de + noun*. I once made the mistake of contracting *de* with a following definite determiner.

French	English
Quand on mange beaucoup de nourriture mexicaine, on se remplit <u>du</u> gaz.	When you eat a lot of Mexican food, you get full of gas.

I was wrong in writing *du* (*de+le=du*). In this case, the preposition *de* is not followed by any determiner, so it does not contract. The correct way of writing this sentence would be:

French	English
Quand on mange beaucoup de nourriture mexicaine, on se remplit de gaz.	When you eat a lot of Mexican food, you get full of gas.

être + Adjective + Preposition

When the structure *être + Adjective* is followed by a preposition, the adjective determines which preposition is used. An adjective of anger calls for *contre*. Most other adjectives call for *de*.

French	English
Je suis content de toi.	I'm happy with/for you.
Elle est fâchée contre eux.	She is angry at them.
La fille est jalouse de son frère.	The girl is jealous of her brother.

à/en

The first set of tricky prepositions that French students begin to learn are *à* and *en*. However, students usually don't learn to use these properly right away, and some students never learn to use them properly.

à (au, aux)	en
-Before masculine countries	-Before feminine countries, states, provinces, continents, etc.
-Before cities and towns	-Before masculine countries, states, and provinces that begin with a vowel.

Examples:
Je vais à Paris. (Paris is a city.)
I'm going to Japan.

Elle va au Japon. (Japan is a masculine country.)
She is going to Japan.

Nous allons aux Etats-Unis. (The US is a masculine country.)
We're going to the United States.

Il va en Ontario. (Ontario is masculine, but it begins with a vowel.)
He's going to Ontario.

Mon ami est allé en France. (France is a feminine country.)
My friend went to France.

avant/devant

Both of these prepositions mean *before*, but they cannot be used interchangeably. *Avant* means *before* in expressions of time, and *devant* means *before* in space. (*Devant* really means *in front of/ahead*, but it can be translated to *before* in certain Shakespearean-like phrases in English.)

Examples:

J'ai besoin de vos devoirs avant 14 heures.
I need your homework before 2:00 PM.

Agenouille-toi devant moi.
Kneel before me.

dans/en

These two prepositions are usually translated to *in* in English, but there are slight differences.
Dans implies that there are limits. In space *dans* means *inside*:

Il y a beacoup d'élèves dans la salle de classe.
There a lot of students in the class.

In expressions of time it refers to future intentions:

Je nettoyerai ma salle dans une heure.
I will clean my room in an hour.

En means *in* in the following cases:

-Before languages (en anglais)
-Any case where *in* doesn't mean *inside*
-*In expressions of time where one expresses the amount of time needed to perform a task

Comment dit-on ça en français?
How do you say this in French?

Elle croit en Dieu.
She believes in God.

*Je nettoyerai ma salle en une heure.
I will clean my room in an hour.
(An hour is the amount of time required to clean the room.)

*Je nettoyerai ma salle dans une heure.
I will clean my room in an hour.
(I will start *to clean my room in an hour.)*

For (pour/ pendant/depuis)

The preposition *for* never translates well into other languages. It can be translated to three different prepositions in French. Here is a chart that explains their functions:

for	usage
pour	recipient/purpose
pendant	complete duration
depuis	incomplete duration

Examples:

J'ai un cadeau pour vous. (recipient)
I have a gift for you.

Elle étudie beaucoup pour réussir à l'examen. (purpose)
She studies a lot in order to pass the test.

Il a plu pendant trois heures. (complete duration)
It rained for three hours.

Je lis ce livre depuis deux heures. (incomplete duration)
I've been reading this book for two hours.

With (avec/à)

The most common translation for *with* is *avec*. But it's also possible to use *à* (*au, aux, à la*). The preposition *avec* means *in the accompaniment of*. The preposition *à* is for descriptions.

French	English
Elle sort avec moi.	*She's going out with me.*
Avez-vous vu la fille aux cheveux blonds?	*Did you see the girl with the blond hair?*

You have probably already been exposed to this construction before. Most students learn the following food related items. It makes use of this particular usage of *à*.

French	English
une glâce au chocolat	*chocolate ice cream*
une glâce à la vanille	*vanilla ice cream*
une glâce à la fraise	*strawberry ice cream*
une tarte aux fraises	*strawberyy ice cream*

On (sur/à)

Sur is the most common translation of *on*. It's also possible to use *à* in certain contexts. Look at the following examples:

French	English
Mon ami est à la télé.	*My friend's on TV.*
Mon ami est sur la télé.	*My friend's on (top of the) TV.*

The *Imparfait* & the *Passé Composé*

Most French students know how to conjugate these two tenses, but they always have trouble deciding which one to use because they both convey past actions. Almost every book on French will tell you the following explanation or something similar: the *imparfait* is used for incomplete actions, and the *passé composé* is used for complete actions. This is true, but it's a little too vague. When I tutor students, I use the acronyms **HIDE** and **STARS**.

Conjugating the *imparfait* is easy. Take the *nous* form of the present indicative, remove the ending *-ons*, and add the appropriate endings.

parler

	Singular	Plural
1	parl*ais*	parl*ions*
2	parl*ais*	parl*iez*
3	parl*ait*	parl*aient*

finir

	Singular	Plural
1	finiss*ais*	finiss*ions*
2	finiss*ais*	finiss*iez*
3	finiss*ait*	finiss*aient*

vendre

	Singular	Plural
1	vend*ais*	vend*ions*
2	vend*ais*	vend*iez*
3	vend*ait*	vend*aient*

There is only one irregular verb in the *imparfait*. (Most grammar books call this verb irregular. But if you look closely at the conjugations, the endings are the same. Only the stem is irregular.)

être

	Singular	Plural
1	ét*ais*	ét*ions*
2	ét*ais*	ét*iez*
3	ét*ait*	ét*aient*

To learn the uses of the *imparfait*, use the acronym **HIDE**.

Habitual actions (used to + verb)
Incomplete actions (was/were + ing form of verb)
Descriptions in the past
Emotions/feelings (most of the time)

Whenever English uses the habitual past (used to + verb), French uses the *imparfait*. Whenever English uses the past progressive (was/were + ing form of verb), French ALWAYS uses the *imparfait*. The *imparfait* is also used to describe things in the past, and it is used when expressing one's emotions. Many French grammar books say that the *imparfait* is used when something happens repeatedly, but this is a flawed explanation. If one said *J'ai lu ce livre* it would require the *passé composé*. According to the flawed explanation, one would have to say *Je lisais ce livre deux fois* if one wanted to say *I read this book twice*. However, this is incorrect. It should be *J'ai lu ce livre deux fois*. When those grammar books say that the *imparfait* is used for actions that happen repeatedly, they mean to say that it is used for habitual actions (used to + verb).

Examples of the *imparfait*:

J'allais toujours au cinéma quand j'étais jeune.
I always went to the movies when I was young.

Elle parlait en espagnol.
She was speaking in French.

Sa voiture était blanche et n'avait que trois pneus.
His car was white and only had three tires.

Je ne me sentais pas bien.
I didn't feel well.

Conjugating the *passé composé* is much more difficult because it requires the use of an auxiliary verb. When conjugating the *passé composé*, you will need to know how to conjugate the verbs *être* and *avoir* in the present tense.

étre

	Singular	Plural
1	suis	sommes
2	es	êtes
3	est	sont

avoir

	Singular	Plural
1	ai	avons
2	as	avez
3	a	ont

You will also need to know how to form past participles. For *er* verbs, remove the *er* and add *é*. For verbs, remove the *ir* and add *i*. For *re* verbs, remove the *re* and add *u*.

Examples:

Infinitive	Past Participle
parler	parlé
finir	fini
vendre	vendu

The following are examples of verbs conjugated in the *passé composé*. The only verb whose past participle is irregular is *être*, i.e. *été*.

parler

	Singular	Plural
1	ai parlé	avons parlé
2	as parlé	avez parlé
3	a parlé	ont parlé

finir

	Singular	Plural
1	ai fini	avons fini
2	as fini	avez fini
3	a fini	ont fini

vendre

	Singular	Plural
1	ai vendu	avons vendu
2	as vendu	avez vendu
3	a vendu	ont vendu

être

	Singular	**Plural**
1	ai été	avons été
2	as été	avez été
3	a été	ont été

The most difficult part of learning the *passé composé* is knowing when to use the verb *avoir* or the verb *être*. Generally speaking, any verb of motion or change requires *être*. Pronominal verbs (often called reflexive verbs) require *être*. Whenever a verb that would usually require *être* has a direct object, *avoir* must be used instead. All other verbs require *avoir*. To learn the verbs that use *être* in the *passé compose*, use the following mnemonic device:

Dr. & Mrs. Vanddertrampp

Descendre Retourner	Mourir Rester Sortir	Venir Arriver Naître Devenir Décéder Entrer Revenir Tomber Rentrer Aller Monter Partir Passer

aller

	Singular	Plural
1	suis allé(e)	sommes allé(e)s
2	es allé(e)	êtes allé(e)(s)
3	est allé(e)	sont allé(e)s

As you can see from the verb chart, any verb that requires *être* must also agree in gender and number.

To learn the uses of the *passé composé*, use the acronym **STARS**.

Sudden occurrence
Time limit/Completed Action
Action disrupts the action of the verb in the imperfect
Reaction to another action
Series of distinct instances

As you can see, all of these fall under the category of "complete action" if we return to our initial explanation of the *passé composé*. But it helps to have clarification like this.

Examples of the *passé composé*:

Il a commencé à pleuvoir.
It started to rain.
(sudden occurence, complete action)

Il a plu pendant deux heures.
It rained for two hours
(time limit)

J'étudiais quand le téléphone a sonné.
I was studying when the phone rang.
(action disrupts action of *imparfait* verb)

Quand mon frère a porté mes chaussures, je me suis fâché.
When my brother wore my shoes, I got mad.
(reaction to another action)

J'ai lu ce livre deux fois.
I read this book twice.
(series of distinct instances)

Decide whether to use the *imparfait* or the *passé composé* in the following sentences. Afterwards, translate them into French.

1. It was raining.

2. I saw my teacher.

3. I was reading a book when I saw a cat.

4. She read this book three times.

5. They didn't come because they were tired.

6. We used to go to the movies all the time.

7. What were you doing?

8. What did you do?

9. It rained for three hours.

10. The house was small and white.

11. I ate there every day.

12. What did you eat?

13. What were you eating?

14. The man was singing in Spanish.

15. The man sang in Spanish.

Aspect

Another way of explaining the differences between the imperfect and the preterit is using the concept of aspect. Imperfective aspect expresses incomplete actions, and perfective aspect expresses complete actions. This is really just a fancy explanation of the definition explained in the beginning of the chapter.

Aspect	Meaning	Tense
Imperfective	Incomplete	*Imparfait*
Perfective	Complete	*Passé Composé*

"What was going on?"/ "What happened?

If the acronyms HIDE and STARS do not work for you, you can ask yourself if the situation you are talking about answers the question *What was going on?* (*imparfait*) or the question *What happened?* (*passé composé*). This is good if the situation cannot be explained in the above rules. For example, if you wanted to say *The cat was eating*, you would immediately know that the imperfect is required because this is an incomplete action (was/were + ing form). But you can also ask yourself if this situation answers one of the above mentioned questions. This situation answers the question *What was going on?*, but it does not answer the question *What happened?* The translation, therefore, is "*Le chat mangeait.*"

Event/State

If you're a really advanced student and/or understand linguistic terminology, you may find Sharon Rand's explanation of the *imparfait* and the *passé composé* more enlightening.

Events are expressed by the *passé composé*. Rand writes that "an event is complete within itself without taking into account that which happens before or after" (Rand, 24).

States are expressed by the *imparfait*. Rand writes that a "state is a complete absence of change" and "that all the phases of the static situation are therefore identical to one another" (Rand, 24).

Indirect Speech/Direct Speech

The *imparfait* is also used for indirect or reported speech. Direct speech is when a speaker is repeating what someone else said verbatim. Indirect speech is when a speaker says what someone else said that is not verbatim. Look at the following sentences.

My sister said, "I am going to France." (direct speech)
Ma soeur m'a dit, "Je vais en France." (direct speech)

My sister said that she was going to France.
(indirect/reported speech)
Ma soeur m'a dit qu'elle allait à France. (indirect/reported speech)

Agreement with Past Participle

If a verb in the *passé composé* (or any other compound tense) has a direct object pronoun, the past participle of the main verb has to agree in gender and number just like an adjective.

J'ai reçu les lettres.
Je les ai reçues.

The past participle has an *e* and an *s* because the word *lettres* is feminine and plural.

If a direct object precedes the verb, the past participle must agree in gender and number.

La femme que j'ai vue était belle.
The woman that (whom) I saw was beautiful.

Plus-que-parfait

The *plus-que-parfait* is a French past tense that is used to express a past action that occurs before another past action or to express *had + past participle*. The *plus-que-parfait* is formed with the imparfait of either avoir or etre. The rules regarding avoir and etre in the plus-que-parfait are the same as they are in the *passé composé*.

Example:

Quand mes amis m'ont téléphoné, j'avais déjà fini tous mes devoirs.

When my friends called me, I had already finished all my homework.

The French Subjunctive

The French subjunctive is probably one the most difficult things that you will ever encounter in French grammar. The subjunctive frustrates many students. It's easy to see why. It has so many uses. I will explain the subjunctive the traditional way and my way. One thing that many students assume about the subjunctive is that it always conveys doubt. This is only one of its many uses.

Conjugating the subjunctive is relatively easy. Take the 3rd person plural form of the present indicative, remove the *ent*, and add the appropriate endings. It is sometimes difficult to tell whether a verb is indicative or subjunctive. For example, the indicative and subjunctive forms of the verb *parler* look exactly the same in the singular forms and the 3rd person plural form.

	sing. (-er)	**plural**	**sing. (-ir)**	**plural**	**sing. (-re)**	**plural**
1	parle	parl*ions*	finisse	finiss*ions*	vendre	vendr*ions*
2	parl*es*	parl*iez*	finiss*es*	finiss*iez*	vendr*es*	vendr*iez*
3	parle	parl*ent*	finisse	finiss*ent*	vendre	vendr*ent*

	être		avoir		faire	
	sing.	**plural**	**sing.**	**plural**	**sing.**	**plural**
1	sois	soyons	aie	ayons	fasse	fassions
2	sois	soyez	aies	ayez	fasses	fassiez
3	soit	soient	ait	aient	fasse	fassent

	aller		savoir		pouvoir	
	sing.	**plural**	**sing.**	**plural**	**sing.**	**plural**
1	aille	allions	sache	sachions	puisse	puissions
2	ailles	alliez	saches	sachiez	puisses	puissiez
3	aille	aillent	sache	sachent	puisse	puissent

vouloir

	sing	**plural**
1	veuille	voulions
2	veuilles	vouliez
3	veuille	veuillent

Usage

To learn the uses of the French subjunctive, use the following acronym: DINNER.

Doubt/Uncertainty
Influence
Non-existence
Negating certain verbs
Emotional reactions
Required conjunctions

Examples of subjunctive:
Je doute qu'il vienne.
I doubt he's coming.

Nous ne sommes pas sûrs que tu aies raison.
We're not sure that you're right.

Elle veut que je m'en aille.
She wants me to go away.

Ma mère me dit que je nettoie ma salle.
My mother tells me to clean my room.

Je suis content que tu sois ici.
I'm glad you're here.

Ils craignent que leur père soit mort.
They fear that their father is dead.

J'étudie toujours à moins que ma petit-fille soit avec moi.
I always study unless my girlfriend is with me.

Mes parents travaillent pour que nous ayons de l'argent.
My parents work so that we have money.

Doubt/Uncertainty

The subjunctive is used with verbs of doubt or uncertainty. It is a common misconception that the subjunctive always conveys a sense of doubt, but this is not the case. It has other uses as well. Some verbs of doubt include, but are not limited to, *douter, ne pas être sûr* and *ne pas être certain.*

Choose the correct form of the verb.

1. Le professeur doute que ses étudiants (font/fassent) leur devoirs.
2. Nous ne doutons pas qu'il y (a/ait) un problem.
3. Je ne suis pas sûr que je (comprends/comprenne).
4. Il est certain que l'école (a/ait) besoin de plus d'argent.
5. Il est possible qu'il (pleut/pleuve).

Influence

The subjunctive is used when a verb in the main clause is influencing the subject in the dependent clause.

Choose the correct form of the verb.

1. Je veux que tu (apprends/aprennes) le français.
2. Ma mère me dit que je (fait/fasse) mes devoirs.
3. Le professeur exige que ses étudiants (vont/aillent) en classe.
4. Mon frère veut que son chien ne (dort/dorme) pas dans son lit.

Non-existence

The subjunctive is used when something isn't known to exist. However, this use of the subjunctive seems to be disappearing. According to one of my French professors, the indicative would normally be used nowadays.

Examples:

Nous cherchons un secretaire qui sache anglais.
We're looking for a secretary who knows English.
(We don't know if such a secretary exists.)

Nous avons un secretaire qui sait anglais.
We have a secretary who knows English.
(We know that such a secretary exists.)

Avez-vous un secretaire qui sache anglais?
Do you have a secretary who knows English?
(We don't know if such a secretary exists.)

Vous avez un secretaire qui sait anglais.
You have a secretary who knows English.
(We know that such a secretary exists.)

Il n'y a personne ici qui sache anglais.
There is nobody here who knows English.
(We know that such a person that DOES NOT exist.)

Choose the correct form of the verb.

1. J'ai besoin d'un étudiant qui (connait/connaisse) bien les ordinateurs.
2. Y a-t-il un professeur ici qui (sait/sache) italien?
3. Nous avons deux étudiants qui (connaient/connaissent) bien les ordinateurs.
4. Il n'y a aucun professeur qui (sait/sache) français.
5. L'étudiante cherche quelqu'un qui (peut/puisse) l'aider avec son français.

Negating Certain Verbs

The subjunctive is used when certain verbs are negated. The most common ones are *penser* and *croire*.

Examples:

Je ne crois pas que tu aies raison.
I don't think that you're right.

Nous ne pensons pas que ce soit une bonne idée.
We don't think that it's a good idea.

The verbs *penser* and *croire* are also used in the subjunctive in questions.

Croyez-vous que je sache la bonne réponse?
Do you think I know the right answer?

Emotional Reactions

The subjunctive is used when describing an emotional reaction to something else.

Examples:
Je suis content que ma sœur vienne.
I'm glad my sister is coming.

Nous craignons que notre chien soit mort.
We fear that our dog is dead.

Choose the correct form of the verb.

1. Nous avons peur que la voiture (est/soit) en panne.
2. Je suis content que tu (viens/viennes) à la fête.
3. Elle est triste que son frère (est/soit) malade.
4. Le professeur est surpris que ses étudiants (apprennent/apprendent) autant.
5. La fille est jalouse que son frère (a/ait) des bonbons.

Required Conjunctions

Certain conjunctions always require the subjunctive.

à moins que	unless
pour que	so that
à fin que	so that
avant que	before
jusqu'à ce que	until
à condition que	provided that
pourvu que	provided that
bien que	even though

Examples:

Nous allons étudier à moins que nos amis viennent.
We're going to study unless our friends come.

Le professeur explique le subjonctif pour que ses étudiants le comprennent.
The professor explains the subjunctive so that his students understand it.

Marie est venue en class bien qu'elle soit malade.
Marie came to class even though she's sick.

When There Is No Change In Subject

When there is no change in subject from the independent verb to the dependent verb, neither the subjunctive nor the indicative is used. Instead, the infinitive is used.

Examples:

Je veux aller au cinema. (The infinitive is used.)
I want to go to the movies.

Je veux que tu ailles au cinema avec moi. (The subjunctive is used.)
I want you to go to the movies with me.

Impersonal Expressions

The subjunctive is required after certain impersonal expressions. Even though most of these expressions fall under a category in the DINNER acronym, it is helpful to have a list of them to look up easily and conveniently.

Il n'est pas certain que_____	It is not certain that_____
Il n'est pas sûr que_____	It is unsure that_____
Il est(n'est pas) possible que_____	It is (im)possible that _____
Il n'est pas probable que_____	It is improbable that _____
Il douteux que _____	It is doubtful that _____

When "que" Changes to "à ce que"

In *Practice Makes Perfect: Advanced French Grammar,* Véronique Mazet explains that certain verbs require more than just *que* when followed by a subjunctive clause. She provides a good list, but she doesn't explain why these verbs require *à ce que* instead of *que*. After analyzing these verbs, I found a pattern. The subjunctive clause seems to express sort of goal. However, if you don't want to memorize these verbs with a rule like this, you can use the following acronym: AVOIR DETTE.

A	s'attendre	to expect
V	veiller	to ensure that
O	s'opposer	to be opposed to
I	s'intéresser	to be interested in
R	se refuser	to refuse to
D	se decider	to make up one's mind
E	être attentive(-ve)	to be attentive
T	tenire	to insist on
T	travailler	to work toward
E	s'employer	to work toward

Examples:

French	English
J'ai tenu à ce qu'il vienne.	*I insisted that he come.*
Le prof veille à ce que ses étudiants réuississent à l'examen.	*The professor ensures that his students pass the exam.*

Read pages 71-72 of Mazet's book on French grammar.

Past Subjunctive

The past subjunctive is used for the same reasons as the present subjunctive, but the action of the second verb occurs before the action of the first verb. The present subjunctive is used if the action of both verbs are simultaneous or if the action of the second verb is to occur in the future.

Examples:

Je ne crois pas qu'il vienne.
I don't think he's coming.

The actions of both verbs are simultaneous in these two sentences.

Je ne crois pas qu'il soit venu.
I don't think he came.

The action of the second verb occurs before the action of the first verb.

Formation

The past subjunctive is formed by taking the present subjunctive of either the verb *avoir* or the verb *être* and adding the past participle of the main verb.

parler

	Singular	Plural
1	aie parlé	ayons parlé
2	aies parlé	ayez parlé
3	ait parlé	aient parlé

finir

	Singular	Plural
1	aie fini	ayons fini
2	aies fini	ayez fini
3	ait fini	aient fini

vendre

	Singular	Plural
1	aie vendu	ayons vendu
2	aies vendu	ayez vendu
3	ait vendu	aient vendu

The verb *être* is used with the Dr. & Mrs. Vandertramp verbs.

aller

	Singular	Plural
1	sois allé(e)	soyons allé(e)s
2	sois allé(e)	soyez allé(e)(s)
3	soit allé(e)	soient allé(e)s

Examples of the past subjunctive:

Je suis heureux que vous soyez venue à ma fête.
I'm glad you came to my party.

Les parents étaient heureux que leur fils aient reçu de bonnes notes.
The parents were happy that their son got good grades.

When There Is No Change In Subject

The past infinitive is used when the action of the second verb occurs before the action of the independent verb.

Je ne crois pas que tu aies assez étudié.
I don't think that you've studied enough.

Je ne crois pas avoir assez étudié.
I don't think that I've studied enough.

Sequence of Tenses/Moods

Independent Verb	Dependent Verb
present indicative	1. present subjunctive 2. past subjunctive
imparfait/passé composé	1. present subjunctive 2. past subjunctive
future	present subjunctive
future perfect	present subjunctive
conditional	present subjunctive

The first column shows the independent verb. The second column shows what form of the subjunctive goes with the verb form in the first column. Although there are more possibilities, these are the most common. If the actions of the two verbs are simultaneous, the present subjunctive is used. If the action of the second verb occurs before the action of the first verb, the past subjunctive is used.

Bringing the Isolated Concepts Together

Each isolated grammatical concept in French isn't difficult in itself. But when two or more grammatical concepts are thrown together, it can cause grammatical chaos. For example, negating isn't difficult. But negating a verb in the *passé composé* can be tricky. And negating a verb in the *passé composé* with a couple of pronouns can be even trickier. This section will show you how to mix these grammatical concepts together in a systematic manner.

Determiners + BAGS Adjectives

When the indefinite and partitive determiners precede a *plural* BAGS adjective, the only acceptable form is *de*. (However, most French speakers tend not to follow this rule.)

Examples:

French	English
Nous avons de grands livres.	We have some big books.
Il y a de jolies femmes ici.	There are some pretty women here.

Negation + Questions

Normally, the *ne...pas* (and other negative constructions) go around the conjugated verb.

Je ne connais pas la réponse.
In questions (only inversions) the negative construction goes around the verb, even with the subject.

Ne savez-vous pas la réponse?

Ne +	VERB+	SUBJECT +	*pas +*	OBJECTS

Negation + Pronouns

When there are pronouns in a negative sentence, the negative construction goes around the conjugated verb as usual, even if there are pronouns.

Je ne l'aime pas.
Elle ne lui dit pas la verité.

SUBJECT +	*ne +*	PRONOUN +	VERBS +	*pas*

Negation + Passé Composé

When a verb is conjugated in the *passé composé*, the negative construction goes around the auxiliary verbs *avoir* and *être*. Many students will often put the second component of the negative construction after the past participle.

Je n'ai pas parlé.
Nous n'avons rien dit.

SUBJECT +	*ne* +	AUX. VERB +	*pas/jamais/plus/rien* +	PAST PART.

The previous structure works *ne...pas, ne...jamais,* and *ne...plus.* It does not work with *ne...rien* or *ne...personne.* The following structure must be used instead.

SUBJECT +	ne +	AUX. VERB +	PAST PART.	personne/aucun(e)

Je n'ai vu personne.
Elle n'a dit aucun mot.

If you're wondering why the structure is different for these two negative constructions, it's that *personne* and *aucun(e)* are being used as direct objects. A direct object has to follow the past participle of a verb in a compound tense such as the *passé composé*.

Negation + Infinitive

When the infinitive is being negated, the *ne...pas* structure doesn't go around it. It is placed directly before it.

Être ou ne pas être, c'est la question.
To be or not to be, that is the question.

Quelquefois, il vaut mieux de ne rien dir.
Sometimes, it's better not to say anything.

When *ne...personne* and *ne...aucun(e)* are used with the infinitive, the *ne* precedes it, and the second element follows it.

Je ne veux voir personne.
I don't want to see anyone.

Il ne sait conjuguer aucun verbe
He doesn't know how to conjugate any verb.

Negation + Pronouns + Infinitive

When an infinitive is negated and contains pronouns, it follows one of these patterns:

ne...pas/jamais/rien	PRONOUN	INFINITIVE

OR

ne	PRONOUN	INFINITIVE	*personne*

Examples:
Il vaut mieux ne pas lui dire la vérité.
It's better not to tell him the truth.

Il vaut mieux ne le voir à personne.
It's better not to show it to anybody.

Pronouns + Passé Composé

SUBJECT+	PRONOUN (DO/IO/y/en) +	AUX. +	PAST PART.

Je lui ai dit la réponse.
Je la lui ai dite.

Since the direct object pronoun is feminine, the past participle has to have an extra *e*. When there is more than one pronoun, they go in the following order:

DO Pronoun +	IO Pronoun +	*y +*	*en*

Negation + Pronouns + Passé Composé

S +	*ne* +	PRONOUN +	AUX. +	*pas* (etc) +	PAST PART.

Il ne l'a pas fait.

Negation + Questions + Pronoun + Passé Composé

Ne	PRONOUN	AUX.	SUBJECT	*pas* (etc) +	PAST PART.

Ne m'avez-vous pas dit la bonne réponse?

Answers to Exercises

Adjectives

1. Mon chien est *meilleur* que ton chien. (bon/plus)

2. Ce livre-ci est *plus grand* que ce livre-là. (grand/plus)

3. La maison est *aussi petit* que les autres maisons. (petit/aussi)

4. Les ordinateurs des années soixante-dix sont *plus lents* que ceux d'aujourd'hui. (lent/plus)

5. Les chats sont *moins stupides* que les chiens. (stupide/moins)

6. Le français est *plus joli* que le russe. (joli/plus)

7. Les langues romances sont *plus jolies* que les langues slaviques. (joli/plus)

Translate the following sentences.

1. We have a bigger house than you (informal).
   Nous avons une plus grande maison que toi.

2. They have a more interesting book than us.
   Ils ont un livre plus intéressant que nous.

3. I have a smarter son than you (formal).
   J'ai un fils plus intelligent que vous.

Determiners

1. I see the car.
    Je vois la voiture.
2. I don't see the car.
    Je ne vois pas la voiture.
3. She wants a horse.
    Elle veut un cheval.
4. She doesn't want a horse.
    Elle ne veut pas de cheval.
5. They would like some coffee.
    Ils voudraient du café.
6. They don't want any coffee.
    Ils ne veulent pas de café.
7. I don't have any money.
    Je n'ai pas d'argent.
8. I don't have any money in my wallet.
    Je n'ai pas d'argent dans ma portefeuille.
9. That's a cat.
    C'est un chat.
10. That's not a cat.
    Ce n'est pas un chat.
11. Are there any questions?
    Y a-t-il des questions?
    Il y a des questions?
12. There aren't any questions.
    Il n'y a pas de questions.
13. The students want a party.
    Les étudiants veulent une fête.
14. The students don't want a test.
    Les étudiants ne veulent pas d'examen.

1. Je veux lire *ce* livre.

2. Elle veut *cette* robe rouge.

3. Il parle à *cet* homme.

4. Je vais lire *ces* livres.

5. Elle a lu *ce* livre.

6. Nous n'aimons pas *ces* règles.

7. *Ce* chien est vieux.

8. *Cette* lumière est brillante.

9. *Ces* voitures sont en panne.

10. Je hais *ce* cours (*sing*).

11. *Cet* ordinateur est très lent.

12. *Ces* ordinateurs sont très lents.

13. Je hais *ces* cours (*plural*).

14. Qu'est-ce que tu fais dans *ce* bâtiment-ci ?

15. *Cette* fois est la dernière fois.

16. *Cette* main est une terrible main de poker.

17. Voulez-vous *ce* crayon-ci ou *ce* crayon-là?

1. my car
   ma voiture
2. your book (informal)
   ton livre
3. her notebook
   son cahier
4. his shirt
   sa chemise
5. our child
   notre enfant
6. our children
   nos enfants
7. your dictionary (formal)
   votre dictionnaire
8. your dictionaries (formal)
   vos dictionnaires
9. your books (informal)
   tes livres
10. their house
    leur maison
11. their houses
    leurs maisons
12. my cars
    mes voitures

1. Il est français.
    Il est français?
    Est-il français?
    Est-ce qu'il est français?
    Il est français, n'est-ce pas?
2. Ils viennent.
    Ils viennent?
    Viennent-ils?
    Est-ce qu'ils viennent?
    Ils viennent, n'est-ce pas?
3. Vous êtes des Etats-Unis.
    Vous êtes des États-Unis?
    Êtes-vous des États-Unis?
    Est-ce que vous êtes des États-Unis?
    Vous êtes des États-Unis, n'est-ce pas?
4. Nous allons en France.
    Nous allons en France?
    Allons-nous en France?
    Est-ce que nous allons en France?
    Nous allons en France, n'est-ce pas?
5. Elles ont la clé.
    Elles ont la clé?
    Ont-elles la clé?
    Est-ce qu'elles ont la clé?
    Elles ont la clé, n'est-ce pas?

1. Where are you from?
     Vous êtes d'où?
     D'où êtes-vous?
     D'où est-ce que vous êtes?
2. How many kids does he have?
     Il a combien d'enfants?
     Combien d'enfants a-t-il?
     Combien d'enfants est-ce qu'il a?
3. Where does Marie work?
     Marie travaille où?
     Où Marie travaille-t-elle?
     Où est-ce que Marie travaille?

1. Nous savons la réponse.
     Nous la savons.
2. J'aime l'ordinateur.
     Je l'aime.
3. J'aime les ordinateurs.
     Je les aime.
4. Ils voient le chemin.
     Ils le voient.
5. Détestez-vous cette voiture?
     La détestez-vous?

1. Il parle à l'homme.
     Il lui parle.
2. Nous donnons des cadeaux à nos enfants.
     Nous leur donnons des cadeaux.
3. Vous parlez à Robert.
     Vous lui parlez.
4. Ils parlent à Marie.
     Ils lui parlent.
5. Je parle à mon professeur.
     Je lui parle.
6. Il montre son tailleur à Chloé.
     Il lui montre son tailleur.

1. Mes chaussures sont blanches, mais *les tiennes/les vôtres* (yours) sont noires.

2. Nos enfants sont grands, mais *les tiens/les vôtres* (yours) sont petits.

3. Ses yeux sont verts, mais *les siens* (hers) sont bleus.

4. Vos étudiants sont intelligents, mais *les miens* (mine) sont un peu stupides.

1. Cette voiture est puissante, mais *celle-ci* est fragile.

2. Ce livre est grand, mais *celui-ci* est petit.

3. Ces cartes sont vielles, mais *celles-ci* sont nouvelles.

4. Ces chevaux sont bruns, mais *ceux-ci* sont blancs.

1. He and I have a lot of money.
   Lui et moi avons beaucoup d'argent.
2. We have something for you. (informal)
   Nous avons quelque chose pour toi.
3. We have something for you. (formal)
   Nous avons quelqe chose pour vous.
4. The book belongs to me.
   Le livre est à moi.
5. *She* is your cousin.
   Elle, elle est ta cousine.
6. It's him.
   C'est lui.
7. She is prettier than her.
   Elle est plus jolie qu'elle.
8. We have more money than you-all.
   Nous avons plus d'argent que vous.
9. I want to go out with him.
   Je veux sortir avec lui.
10. He wants to go out with her.
    Il veut sortir avec elle.

1. Il y a deux livres.
   Il y en a deux.
2. Elle va au cinema.
   Elle y va.
3. Nous jouons du football.

Nous en jouons
4. L'université a beaucoup d'étudiants.
   L'université en a beaucoup.
5. Il a trois frères.
   Il en a trois.
6. Je voudrais du soda.
   J'en voudrais.

1. It was raining.
   Il pleuvait.
2. I saw my teacher.
   J'ai vu mon prof.
3. I was reading a book when I saw a cat.
   Je lisais un livre quand j'ai vu un chat.
4. She read this book three times.
   Elle a lu ce livre trois fois.
5. They didn't come because they were tired.
   Ils ne sont pas venus parce qu'ils étaient fatigués.
6. We used to go to the movies all the time.
   Nous allions au cinéma tout le temps.
7. What were you doing?
   Qu'est-ce que vous fasiez?
8. What did you do?
   Qu'est-ce que vous avez fait?
9. It rained for three hours.
   Il a plu pendant trois heures.
10. The house was small and white.
    La maison était petite et blanche.
11. I ate there every day.
    J'y mangeais tous les jours.
12. What did you eat?
    Qu'est-ce que vous avez mange?
13. What were you eating?
    Qu'est-ce que vous mangiez?
14. The man was singing in Spanish.
    L'homme chantait en espagnol.
15. The man sang in Spanish.
    L'homme a chanté en espagnol.

1. Le professeur doute que ses étudiants (font/*fassent*) leur devoirs.
2. Nous ne doutons pas qu'il y (*a*/ait) un problem.
3. Je ne suis pas sûr que je (comprends/*comprenne*).
4. Il est certain que l'école (*a*/ait) besoin de plus d'argent.
5. Il est possible qu'il (pleut/*pleuve*).

1. Je veux que tu (apprends/*aprennes*) le français.
2. Ma mère me dit que je (fait/*fasse*) mes devoirs.
3. Le professeur exige que ses étudiants (vont/*aillent*) en classe.
4. Mon frère veut que son chien ne (dort/*dorme*) pas dans son lit.

1. J'ai besoin d'un étudiant qui (connait/*connaisse*) bien les ordinateurs.
2. Y a-t-il un professeur ici qui (sait/*sache*) italien?
3. Nous avons deux étudiants qui (*connaient*/connaissent) bien les ordinateurs.
4. Il n'y a aucun professeur qui (sait/*sache*) français.
5. L'étudiante cherche quelqu'un qui (peut/*puisse*) l'aider avec son français.

Recommended Books

Barron's French Grammar
Christopher Kendris, Ph.D.

Barron's French Verbs
Christopher Kendris, Ph.D.

Essential French Grammar
Seymour Resnick

The French Imparfait and Passé Simple in Discourse
Sharon Rebecca Rand

Grammaire Française
Jacqueline Olivier

An Introduction to French Pronunciation (Revised Edition)
Glanville Price

Practice Makes Perfect: Advanced French Grammar
Véronique Mazet

Practice Makes Perfect: French Verb Tenses
Trudie Maria Booth

Bibliography

Mazet, Véronique. Practice Makes Perfect: Advanced French Grammar. 1st ed. New York: McGraw-Hill, 2008.

Rand, Sharon Rebecca. The French Imparfait and Passé Simple in Discourse. 1st ed. Arlington: The Summer Institute of Linguistics and the University of Texas at Arlington, 1993.

Printed in Great Britain
by Amazon.co.uk, Ltd.,
Marston Gate.